HOW TO
FAIL AS
A POPSTAR

VIVEK SHRAYA

HOW TO FAIL AS A POPSTAR

a play

ARSENAL PULP PRESS
VANCOUVER

ARSENAL PULP PRESS
Suite 202 – 211 East Georgia St.
Vancouver, BC V6A 1Z6
Canada
arsenalpulp.com

The publisher gratefully acknowledges the support of the Canada Council for the Arts and the British Columbia Arts Council for its publishing program, and the Government of Canada, and the Government of British Columbia (through the Book Publishing Tax Credit Program), for its publishing activities.

Arsenal Pulp Press acknowledges the xʷməθkʷəy̓əm (Musqueam), Sḵwx̱wú7mesh (Squamish), and səl̓ilwətaʔɬ (Tsleil-Waututh) Nations, custodians of the traditional, ancestral, and unceded territories where our office is located. We pay respect to their histories, traditions, and continuous living cultures and commit to accountability, respectful relations, and friendship.

"Greatest Love of All." Words by Linda Creed, music by Michael Masser © 1977 (renewed) EMI Gold Horizon Music Corp. and EMI Golden Torch Music Corp. Exclusive print rights administered by Alfred Music. All rights reserved. Used by permission of Alfred Music.

Cover and text design by Jazmin Welch
Cover photograph by Heather Saitz
Photographs by Dahlia Katz
Copy edited by Shirarose Wilensky
Proofread by Alison Strobel

Printed and bound in Canada

Library and Archives Canada Cataloguing in Publication:
Title: How to fail as a popstar : a play / Vivek Shraya.
Names: Shraya, Vivek, 1981– author.
Identifiers: Canadiana (print) 2020032456X | Canadiana (ebook) 20200324853 |
  ISBN 9781551528427 (softcover) | ISBN 9781551528434 (HTML)
Subjects: LCSH: Shraya, Vivek, 1981-—Drama.
Classification: LCC PS8637.H73 H69 2021 | DDC C812/.6—dc23

For Whitney Houston,
whose voice made a brown queer kid in Edmonton
believe in my own voice,

Madonna,
for showing me the power of pop,

and Shamik,
for being the original believer.

I decided long ago
Never to walk in anyone's shadows
If I fail, if I succeed
At least I'll live as I believe

—Whitney Houston, "Greatest Love of All"

FOREWORD

I can recall the moment, in the summer of 2018, when Vivek called me with The Pitch. It went something like this:

"Hi. So I have this idea for a play called *How to Fail as a Popstar*. What I am imagining …"

I can't really remember what she said after that. She had sold me with the title alone and my mind was already focused on how to make it happen.

At that point, I had known Vivek for almost a decade. She was initially one of my early social media friends. We followed each other on various platforms, liked each other's posts and pics, and exchanged the occasional message. I remember being quite struck by her social media presence. She was one of the first people I felt was really *using* social media as a tool for self-expression. She took it seriously, long before most of us caught on to what this technology offered. Early on, she understood its power to create a mediated "pop" version of the self.

When I finally got to meet Vivek in person, I was somewhat surprised by her shy, contained, and, dare I say, understated demeanour. Yet a fierceness was present behind her eyes. It lurked in the seriousness with which she spoke of things. As I got to know her better through her performances at Buddies in Bad Times, photo shoots at my apartment with my husband, and various events around town, she began to let down her guard. I began to see the rawness of her hunger for self-realization through art, and I caught glimpses of the pain she carried of an unfulfilled story. It was a pain that I had inside me, too.

This was before her novels, her books of poetry, her talk show appearances, her modelling, and her emergence as a bona fide *icon*. Typically, a person's ascent to any kind of public adulation is accompanied by the rejection of any past "failures." If they are acknowledged at all, they are reframed as stepping stones towards a truer, more real purpose—the necessary stumbling blocks that help sharpen an artist's ultimate and authentic greatness. But with the title *How to Fail as a Popstar*, Vivek was pitching a play that was a refusal to fall into that trope. And this was what hooked me, because fuck that trope.

Working on this play taught me a lot. I learned not only a ton about Vivek—perhaps more than she would ever want me to know—but also a ton about living with failure. Here are the top three lessons that I learned from Vivek about failure:

1. Let go of having to feel good about failure.

Like illness and death (and, quite frankly, most intense human experiences), our society is unable to cope with the real emotional consequences of failure. It compulsively denies our failures by turning them into "life lessons" or "opportunities for growth." Just google "failure + quote" to see how society tells us to manage failure. With this play, Vivek is resisting what is deeply dehumanizing about the social negation of our failures. Our failures are real. The emotions they cause are real. The consequences in our lives and our bodies are real.

May we please be allowed to own our failures!

2. Our dreams need funerals.

Once we can fully own our failures, then the real work of what to do with them can happen. Vivek suggests that our failed ambitions need funerals. They deserve the eulogies, the caskets, the wakes, the awkward conversations, the bad food, the solitary cries, the collective tears, and the burial. The act of mourning is how we, as human beings, process pain. Our failed dreams deserve this process.

3. You gotta keep showin' up.

So, you've owned your failure and you've laid your dream to rest. What's next?

I don't know. Vivek doesn't know.

But what I learned from Vivek's play is that life goes on, and this gives you a choice: you can keep on showing up in your life, or you can stop.

The play does not tell us if showing up will lead to greater happiness in life. But if, like Vivek, you have a life force that is driven by a deep hunger for something *more*, something *bigger*, then you need to keep feeding that hunger. Even if that hunger has caused you pain. Showing up won't satiate that hunger. It won't lead you to the destination you dreamed of. But it will take you somewhere.

And for the Viveks of this world, somewhere is better than nowhere.

Brendan Healy
Artistic director at Canadian Stage
November 2020

Hi everyone! Sorry to interrupt. My name is Vivek Shraya. Before we get started I just want to clarify something. When I say that I failed as a popstar, this is what I mean:

I did not become God.

I did not become Madonna.

None of my music broke into the mainstream.

And I never got to perform on the world's biggest stages—no offence Canadian Stage.

Okay, that's it!

THE POPSTAR

Music Ur the 1

I learned to sing to please my mother
I learned to sing to please God
I learned to sing to please the pretty girls

But along the way
I fell in love
With music—for music's sake
With melody
Now every breath I take, I'm gonna make

Music, music, music, music, music
Cause music ur the 1

I tried to sing to please the people
I tried to win all their love
I tried to sing, but no one stopped to hear

So I disappeared
And fell out of love
With music—for music's sake

With melody
Until I find my way back, I'm gonna make

Music, music, music, music, music
Cause music ur the 1
Music ur the 1, ur the 1
Music ur the 1, ur the 1
Music ur the 1, ur the 1
Music ur the 1, ur the 1

I am twenty-seven years old. In my hand is a first-class ticket. I have never flown first class before. Just a few months ago, I signed a *record deal* with a label in France. And now they've paid for my plane ticket to play a string of shows in Paris. After I settle into my window seat, I can feel the tears filling my eyes. All of my hard work has paid off.

I'm finally crossing over.

THE MAIDEN

Early one morning, just as the sun was rising
I heard a maid sing in the valley below

My earliest memory of music is this song. My mother used to sing it to wake up my brother and me in the morning, while she swung open our bedroom doors and drew our curtains.

Oh don't deceive me, oh never leave me,
How could you use a poor maiden so?

Because I was too young to know what a maiden was, I often imagined my mother as the protagonist of this song. And yet, my mother was nothing like the tragic, desperate maiden. Instead, our relationship straddled the line between love and fear—where she was extremely caring to overcompensate for the unreliability of my father and, perhaps for the very same reason, ever stirring a cauldron of anger that could erupt at any moment. I wanted to do whatever I could to win her love and keep her anger at bay because with anger came violence. Except we never called it that. Smacking your kid around is normal in a brown home.

Also normal in our home was my parents continuously arguing about money. My dad had an enormous debt, which he had accrued, in part, from his extensive pop record collection.

While my dad played Madonna's "La Isla Bonita" on repeat, my brother and I would dance in our living room crammed with *my mother's* collection of goods: bronze statues, an onyx chessboard, and artificial flower arrangements. My mother's logic seemed to be that if we filled our house with shiny things, maybe no one would notice that we weren't rich. It was here, in our ostentatious living room, that I was inducted into singing.

I'm five years old, crouched on the carpet, next to the polished coffee table. My mother is sitting on the velour couch, which is protected by a bedsheet. She hands me a piece of paper with non-English words written on it. I know it's her handwriting because she only writes in caps lock. She tells me that this is a bhajan, then sings a line, and instructs me to repeat after her. She sings another line, and again, I repeat after her.

I don't know why we're doing this. I don't know what these words mean. But I know from her dedication to teaching me that these words are important to her. That me singing them pleases her, soothes her.

THE GURU

Our religious organization centred on an Indian guru named Sai Baba. So the organization was neatly referred to as the "Sai Centre." Except we weren't really a centre. We were a nomadic group of 50 to 100 people, who often rented high school gyms for our Sunday bhajan ceremonies. We would convert them by stretching white sheets on the floor, erecting a life-size photo of Sai Baba under the basketball hoop, and placing a velvet chair beside the photo for him to telepathically sit on.

It was here that I learned that Sai Baba is God, and he had come to remind us that we are God, too. I also learned that we could remember our godliness by singing bhajans. This was pretty convenient because I was often asked to be a lead singer of one of the bhajans.

The person who decided who was allowed to be a lead singer at the Sai Centre was Aunty Jaya. She would point at you when you walked into the gym, which meant: you were chosen. She was a towering woman, always in a sari, who looked like a football player. Her stature, combined with her selecting power and her gruff personality, made her a highly revered and equally disliked character at the centre. But, my God, when she sang, you wouldn't know that voice came out of that woman. She could make an actual football player weep with her smooth, crisp delivery. She was the one I looked up to the most, the one I wanted to sing like. Because when she did, I swear I could feel my own divinity.

I can't think of a better boot camp for learning how to sing than the Sai Centre. When you're singing a bhajan, the main objective is to reach God. Can you imagine the kind of feeling you would squeeze into every vowel and consonant when this is the goal?

Govinda Madhava Gopala Keshava

I loved the intention that was required when singing bhajans, along with their expansive melodies and melodramatic lyrics about being an orphan, a hopeless servant, a passionate seeker. In bhajan lyrics, something is always missing in you, but the fix, the filling, is clear: God.

Jaya Nanda Mukunda Nanda Govinda Radhe Gopala

Unlike math questions that were forever unsolvable, singing a bhajan was asking a question with an answer already embedded into it. And unlike math, not only was this something I could do, I was being told I could do it well. Not only by being chosen by Aunty Jaya but also by others in the congregation. Like the couple who told me that they would drive in from Sherwood Park, outside of Edmonton, just to hear me sing.

Giridhari Giridhari Jaya Radhe Gopala
Ghana Shyama Shyama Shyama Jaya Jaya Radhe Gopala

After the forty minutes of bhajan singing was over, a member of the community would stand up and give a speech on one of the five human values: truth, righteousness, peace, love, and non-violence.

Because of how well I sang, I was soon offered the opportunity to give one of these speeches. Children were seldom asked to do this, but when they were, it was beyond adorable hearing a preaching child. But I wasn't interested in being adorable; I wanted to be different. I loved the element of surprise. So in my speeches I would include snippets of pop covers. For instance, when I spoke about God's unwavering reliability, I also sang a verse from Mariah Carey's version of "I'll Be There."

The adults were always impressed by my "creativity," but mostly in that unspecific "Wow, good job" kind of way. But one night, one of the men in the organization said to me, "I really loved that song you wrote." Uncle Kamal was a reserved man, so I was taken aback by his forwardness. "Oh, I didn't write that song."

I had never considered the possibility of writing my own songs before. But after Uncle Kamal had planted the seed, I began sampling the opening bars of pop songs with my double-deck cassette player and writing devotional songs over the samples. Like this song that I wrote and sang for Lord Rama's birthday at the Sai Centre over Sarah McLachlan's "Fumbling towards Ecstasy."

Beloved blue skin
Grant me permission
To swim in your ocean
Of mercy and compassion
Rama Rama Rama Rama Rama Rama Ram Ram
Rama Rama Rama Rama Rama Rama Ram Ram

THE PRETTY GIRLS

The schooling I received in junior high didn't happen in the classroom but in the hallway.

Lesson 1: Apparently, I was a geek. I hadn't yet developed the required self-consciousness to pay attention to what everyone was wearing, and then dress like them.

Lesson 2: I was also a faggot—which my classmates and random kids liked to repeatedly point out. So helpful!

Coming up with a strategy to make friends became crucial. I began to pay close attention to the *songs* that Lizzie Nickel and Zoey Lane would gush about in class. Lizzie was a super-extroverted white girl who dressed like Kris Kross. Remember them? Zoey was mostly notable for being Lizzie's sidekick. She was Kross to Lizzie's Kris. They were two of my classmates who were actually nice to me. And by "nice," I mean they didn't call me faggot.

After hearing them rave about Mary J. Blige, I made my mom drive me to the Edmonton Public Library so I could take out the Mary J. Blige cassette *What's the 411?*. I learned that album inside out.

The next time Lizzie and Zoey passed by my locker, I quietly hummed Mary's "Real Love." This was a wildly successful endeavour.

"OH MY GOD, I LOVE THAT SONG! I didn't know he could sing like that!"

Soon after, Lizzie and Zoey started introducing me to all their friends, who were also impressed by my singing. By the end of junior high, the most popular girl in the entire school, Melissa Bliss, invited me to sing a duet with her at the school assembly.

Melissa was the only one who got to sing at school assemblies. She always did a Paula Abdul song, with her pouty lips sparkling with tinted gloss, while the jocks would cheer and whistle. Perhaps they were trying to drown out her voice? Because here's the thing: straight up, Melissa was a *terrible* singer. So imagine my frustration being asked to sing at the school assembly—but with Melissa.

And then, she casts herself in the role of a dramatic Madonna, singing the lead in "Take a Bow" and forces *me* to sing the boring male backup part. Despite this, while we sing onstage, *I smile* at Melissa, and at all of my new girlfriends in the audience.

I hear one of the jocks yell, "Faggot!" My voice cracks. I can feel my face heat up. But then I notice Lizzie. She turns around and whacks the jock's knee. Then she winks at me. And I keep singing.

THE JUDGE

Before *American Idol* there was a very important talent competition called "Youth Talent Quest" that took place in Edmonton's most beloved spaces: shopping malls.

Yes, malls, plural. Believe it or not, there's more than the Big One. But there is a hierarchy, which was made clear by the way that the competition started in the smaller malls. If you were successful, you would get to compete against the lucky semifinalists from across the city in West Edmonton Mall's biggest food court. The final rounds took place at Klondike Days, Edmonton's summer exhibition.

The first time I tried out, I decided to sing an a cappella version of an Annie Lennox song that my grandmother loved when I sang it around the house. She happily came to the talent show at Mill Woods Town Centre, our neighbourhood mall, along with my brother and mother, who sat in the back row of chairs in front of the makeshift stage. I sang my heart out for my grandmother in the audience, and for the HMV that loomed in the corner of my eye. When I made it to the next round, I was convinced that it was because of my grandmother's power.

Sitting in West Ed's central food court during the semifinals, with the hybrid smells of TacoTime, New York Fries, and Edo swirling around us, I watched girl after girl get up onstage to painfully belt out "Black Velvet" by Alannah Myles or Mariah's "Hero," with a soulless instrumental always playing in the background. I also studied the group of older women judges wearing floral blouses with shoulder pads to get a sense of what impressed them. They were "industry experts," which often meant they were local singing teachers. And even though I didn't know who they were, as I made my way through the maze of food court tables towards the stage, all dressed up in my dad's office clothes, I was certain I would blow their minds. I was a boy. I was going to sing a cappella. And I was going to sing the ballad from Alanis Morissette's *Jagged Little Pill*—"Mary Jane"—not the obvious single.

When I sang her lyrics about being in the wrong direction, I thought it would be super cool and unpredictable to literally act out being *in the wrong direction*. Away from the audience and towards the public washrooms. I didn't make it to the next round.

The following time I competed, I actually made it to Klondike Days. I chose to sing R.E.M.'s song "You" from their new, aggressive album, *Monster*. I wore a white kurta, with sandalwood prayer beads wrapped around my wrist, and was barefooted. Backstage, the contestants and the MC kept staring at my feet, as though there was some deep message hidden in my absent socks. I didn't make it to the next round.

The last year I competed in Youth Talent Quest, I had finally reached the age limit of nineteen. At the semifinals, I opted to sing an original song I had written called "Madrid." I wore all black, with my sleeves safety-pinned above my shoulders the way Madonna was doing at the time. I had my girlfriend, Sabrina, handwrite a series of my lyrics from the tips of my fingers all the way up my arm, in rows. I accompanied myself on guitar.

I was voted by the judges to move to the final round at K-Days. I decided it was time to get feedback from one of them.

"Excuse me. Is there something I could be doing to improve my performance?"

The judge looked at me in the eye, took a deep breath, and said, "Have you ever considered wearing leather pants?"

The truth is—I had *not* considered wearing leather pants. Nor had I considered that the absence of leather pants was the cause for my repeated losses.

Reading the confusion on my face, the judge offered, "You know, like Ricky Martin ..."

I'm a fag 4 U

They used to call me fag
They used to call me

So I put my sex away
I put my sex away

Then you came
You restored my name
And now, I'm a fag 4 u

My shorts are not high enough
And my shirt is not tight enough
And my sins are not deep enough

Cause I'm a fag, I'm a fag, I'm a fag, I'm a fag

After I released my first album, I won an award for best new artist. This was the speech I gave. It was televised, so you can find it online.

Oh man.

I didn't prepare a speech and I'm sorry, but I'm glad I didn't because I'm not gonna do this like everybody else does it. 'Cause everybody that I should be thanking—I'm really sorry—but I have to use this time. See, Maya Angelou said that we, as human beings, at our best, can only create opportunities. And I'm gonna use this opportunity the way that I want to use it.

So, what I want to say is—everybody out there that's watching, everybody that's watching this world—this world is bullshit. And you shouldn't model your life about what you think that we think is cool and what we're wearing and what we're saying and everything. Go with yourself. Go with yourself ...

And it's just stupid that I'm in this world, but you're all very cool to me, so thank you very much. Bye.

Actually, this never happened.

Well it did happen. To Fiona Apple. At the MTV VMA Awards. I was sixteen when I watched this on TV. Fiona was almost twenty years old. I, too, thought that it was just stupid that I was in this world.

I also remember thinking to myself—*Okay, I have only four years to make it big.*

THE PRODUCER

After class at the university, I would often visit Sabrina at Southgate mall, where she worked at the MAC store.

One day, one of the other MAC artists approaches me, intimidating as fuck. She is dressed head to toe in a long black Stevie Nicks draping dress, and her height is intensified by her modern black beehive. Her eyebrows are sharply drawn in.

"*You*. You sing. I was a judge at a competition you sang at. I'm a singer, too. My name is Elise."

Oh no. Is she going to recommend leather pants, too?

"Listen, your voice is great, but you have talent. Those competitions aren't meant for someone like you." She points her manicured finger at me and says, "You need a *producer*."

Elise tells me that I need to make an album. Of my own songs. She knows just the man to help me do it. It's the same man who has produced her album *Done Up Right*. She scribbles the name "Matt G" and a phone number on the inside of a used lipstick box. "Call him."

I arrange to meet Matt G at his place. As I drive there, I keep thinking: *I'm going to a* producer's *house.* When he opens the door, he bends to greet me because of his height. He leads me down a staircase, through a doorway guarded by a red sheet, into his basement studio. He hands me a guitar and says, "Play me a song."

There's no one at home
I'm all alone
No one to make me feel better

There's no one to call
No one at all
No one to make this weight lighter

I try to pull myself up, pull myself out of this mess

I try not to make eye contact as I sing for him, but I notice him scrunching his eyes. Does he hate my song? After I finish, I hand him back his guitar. He doesn't say anything for a while.

Finally, he tells me that I'm *the one.* He tells me he believes in my talent so much that the album we make together can't just be another album he records in his basement. He tells me that my album could go all the way, which is code for *record deal.* And because he kind of looks like Jim Cuddy, the lead singer of Blue Rodeo—white, wise, kind, and like a rock star in his own right—I believe him.

Going all the way will require recording at the fancy local studio. He tells me that said studio has the best vintage mics—"better than my shitty home studio mics," he says—that will be especially perfect for capturing my voice. These words are kryptonite for a singer and inspire the title for my yet-to-be-recorded first album: *Throat*. A tribute to my voice.

When we crunch the numbers, the album will cost me an estimated $20,000. Where the fuck am I going to get $20,000 from? I start looking into taking out a loan, and of course, the bank wants a co-signer because I'm a twenty-one-year-old university student, living with my parents, working a part-time, minimum-wage job as a receptionist at a hair salon. This means that after hearing my parents fight every day about bills for the house, car, school, braces, while also asserting that music is *not* a legitimate career path, I had to find the audacity to ask my mom if she would co-sign a loan for me to record a $20,000 "hobby."

I don't remember asking her or what her response was. All I remember is driving to the TD Bank on Whyte Ave. and sitting side by side as we signed the dozens of loan forms in silence.

Before Matt G and I started recording the album, he suggested that we book two weeks of pre-production in his basement to create rough versions of the songs. This would save time and money when we were at the official studio. I would sing him one of my songs a cappella, play him a music reference, and then he would turn around and instantly program a loop—and say, "How about this?" Or pump out bass line—"How about this?" I was hyper-intimidated by his one-man show. Every so often, when I would pause to reflect on whether or not we were heading in the right direction, he would go, "Fuck! Shit! Fuck!" Not at me but at the computer—which felt like the same thing. I didn't want to be a diva, or an inflexible artist, so I kept my reservations to a minimum. Plus, he was the producer, which meant he was the expert, right?

There was one time when Matt G asked me, "Hey, do you know anyone who plays the sitar?" Did Matt G secretly want to make a world music album? I shut down that conversation *so* fast.

Once we got into the studio, we had to record drums, bass, guitars, and keyboards first. This ate up more time than what had been allotted for them. The two days allotted to recording my vocals were skimmed down to half a day.

"Don't worry!" Matt G would say as each day passed. "You're a pro. You'll nail the vocals quickly."

As I tried vintage mic after vintage mic in the last few hours of the studio sessions, my voice sounded too tinny, too nasally, too flat.

"You know, sometimes the best mic is that shitty home studio mic," Matt G said.

And so I ended up recording my vocals in his basement after all.

There's this quote: "Talking about music is like dancing about architecture." This is true. But for a young musician, there might be no greater skill than the ability to articulate the music that you're hearing in your head. The music I was hearing was a cross between the Neptunes and Timbaland, two of the hottest producers of that time. You couldn't turn on the radio without hearing a song touched by them, working with artists like Aaliyah, Jay-Z, Britney Spears, Nelly Furtado, and Usher.

But my first album, *Throat*, sounded like a shitty imitation of shitty Canadian rock. It also cost closer to $25,000 to make because of the unbudgeted pre-production sessions and the days of recording final vocals in Matt G's basement studio. My mother and I never discussed the album.

A year later, my arch nemesis released his brand-new solo album. Half of his album was produced by the Neptunes, and the other half by ... yup ... Timbaland. A split-production album by these two mega producers had never existed before ... outside of my head. Until now. My arch nemesis made the exact album I wanted to make.

This wasn't a new dynamic for us. Some of you might have heard of him? Justin Timberlake? Justin and I go way back ... all the way back to the Mickey Mouse Club. You probably didn't know that I was in the Mickey Mouse Club. That's because I'm not white. The only time I got put on TV was when Justin or Christina or Ryan Gosling took a sick day.

I Won't Envy 2.0

Do you know what it's like to want to dance
In somebody else's light?
Do you know what it's like to want to rock
With somebody else's mic?

Don't mean to be so green
Don't mean to be so blue
A lifetime spent in blending in will do that to you

I need a beat, a groove to dance in my own shoes
I won't envy, I won't envy
I need a beat, a groove to dance in my own shoes
I won't envy, I won't envy

THE ROCK STAR

After we finished recording *Throat* in the summer, Matt G began sending it out to "some contacts," putting out "some feelers." In the meantime, I played the album for my friends—all of whom were startled after hearing a few minutes. "It just doesn't sound like you" was the polite response I got over and over again. Panicked, I asked Matt G if he could help me record a bunch of acoustic tracks in his basement studio—just me, voice, and guitar. Something for me to sell at my shows, and drum up interest while we waited for his contacts to get back to him. I named this project *Samsara: The Sketches*.

My friends seemed relieved to hear it, which made me relieved, and audience members were excited to own it. But in the back of my mind, I kept thinking about how *Samsara* had cost me only $500 to make. Why didn't I just do this to begin with?

It turns out that Matt G's "contacts" were just *one* contact: Ian Taylor. Ian Taylor was the booker for one of the most prestigious music venues in Edmonton at the time: the Sidetrack Cafe. He knew every major act that came into town.

And so, four months after recording *Throat*, through Ian, and however many degrees of separation, I get a phone call. Guess who it is?

Timbaland!

No, I wish. It was actually John Wozniak. The lead singer of Marcy Playground. Do you remember that song "Sex and Candy"?

He wasn't really the demographic that I imagined attracting. But here was a bona fide rock star on the phone telling me that he'd heard *Throat*, that he loved the album—which he referred to as "a demo"—that he could make the necessary adjustments to take it to the next level, that he could introduce me to all the right people. And that I needed to get out of Edmonton. "Why don't you come out here to Toronto so we can meet," he said.

Soon after, I get a message from his manager, Carla, setting up my first visit to Toronto and offering to pick me up at the airport. Carla was in her late thirties, sported a drugstore-red bob and bangs, and loved to tell stories. Like how she watched the Twin Towers go down on her bedroom TV, while Ian Taylor fucked the shit out of her. Or how much she wanted to do coke off the bare asses of NSYNC. All of them. Or all of the Canadian celebrities that she knew, including Greig Nori, Sum 41's manager, whom she introduces me to when she takes me on a tour of the iconic Metalworks Studios, where Prince, Guns N' Roses, and Bruce

Springsteen have recorded. Amidst all this, she tells me that she also loves my album, which she proves by blasting it in her leased Lexus.

When we meet with John, *Carla* tells me, "You need to get the fuck out of Edmonton. You can stay on my couch until you sort yourself out." Then she and John begin to *strategize* what they would do once I moved: book a showcase at Canadian Music Week, tweak a handful of the songs from *Throat*, and shop the tracks to labels for a record deal.

I didn't need a lot of coaxing. I had wanted to get out of Edmonton for most of my teenage years, and the timing was perfect: I had just finished university, and finished recording an album that people were hearing and talking about without it even being released. Driving through Toronto's frenetic streets, I knew this was where my dreams would come true.

When I return home, my mom is in the laundry room, and she says, "I know. You're moving, aren't you?" And then we both cried together. I felt enormously guilty because in my culture, you don't leave your family unless you're going to build a new family.

Three weeks after my trip to Toronto, I was back on a flight with two suitcases and two boxes filled with my entire life.

It was all happening.

THE MANAGER

The first mistake I made when I moved to Toronto was agreeing to live in Carla's apartment until I got settled. Her apartment had the kind of furniture you would expect from a music industry mover and shaker—black bookshelves, black leather couches, glass coffee table—but it smelled like a pub.

The second mistake I made was not doing any proper research into what neighbourhood Carla lived in. In my defence, Google Maps didn't exist at the time, but it turned out that she actually lived in Mississauga.

The third mistake I made was telling Carla that my mom had started referring to Carla as "Mama Carla," as a gesture of transference. I think it was comforting to my mom, that if I was going to leave her, at least I would be living with this older woman who was going to take care of me. Mama Carla took a shine to her new name, which she began to use in third person: "Did you see the swiss chicken Mama Carla got us for dinner?"

A few days after I landed, Mama Carla managed to book me a last-minute slot at Canadian Music Week. To drum up interest for the show, as promised, she and John from Marcy Playground took me into record companies to showcase for execs. They'd play some of the album, and then I would sing live. This was a really big deal. Even now, looking back, I realize how rare of an experience that was. Very few aspiring musicians end up in record company offices.

The execs listened poker-faced, and before they could comment, Mama Carla would jump in: "Isn't he *amazing*?"

I would notice them cringe from her pushiness. Then they would smile and nod at me and ask if we could send them more songs.

"Oh, there's definitely more. Just you wait!"

One week later, I meet with John at his studio for him to revamp my songs. Mama Carla is also hanging out with us. At one point in the session, John suggests changing one of my lyrics—from the word "like" to the word "want." A simple change. But then I explain how the song is meant to be about the moment *before* desire kicks in, about an initial interest. "That makes sense," he says.

After a few hours, Mama Carla and I leave the studio. As soon as we get home, she flings her purse on the couch and starts screaming: *"Who the fuck do you think you are? Do you know that there are thousands of artists who are more talented than you, with better voices than you, who are better looking than you? Who the fuck do you think you are? An Indian singer is never going to get signed in this country. So if John Wozniak tells you to change a lyric, you change your fucking lyric."*

It seemed like the transference my mom had hoped for had happened because the only person who had ever come close to yelling at me like this was my own mother.

While Mama Carla continues to yell, I panic. I had just moved to a city where I knew no one, and was living with a woman who was revealing herself to be volatile. I go to bed, telling myself that maybe this outburst was just a one-off.

The next morning, Mama Carla promises to take me on a surprise trip for my birthday that weekend. Was this her way of making amends? For my first ever birthday away from home and loved ones, we drive *by* Niagara Falls and straight into the casino parking lot. Inside, Mama Carla tells me that my birthday present is getting to pull her slot machine handle.

The fourth and final mistake I made was telling Mama Carla that my friends thought I gave good back rubs. Over the next few months, when I'd ask her if she had followed up with a record company after our meeting, or after a press kit had been sent out, she would push out her shoulders and say, "You know, Mama Carla's back is really sore today. Maybe after you give Mama Carla a back rub she can follow up."

What would you do if you were me?

I rubbed the fuck out of that woman's back. Over and over and over again.

One day after she came home from doing errands, she yelled, "Mama Carla has a present for us!" When I got to the door, she was swinging a Lush cosmetics bag and pulled out a container of foot cream. "Mama Carla needs a foot massage."

After five months, I was still living in Mama Carla's apartment. I began to feel hopeless, which was tied to being jobless. But my unemployment was not from lack of trying. After Mama Carla would finish online gambling at three a.m., cradling a two-litre of Diet Coke as she zombie-walked to bed, she would let me use her computer. I would stay up into the early hours and apply for job after job after job. I got so anxious from spending my days just hoping that an employer would call me that I started to deliberately sleep in until five p.m. I stopped taking showers and brushing my teeth because what was the point?

In the evenings, I found myself in the self-help and new age aisles of the Mississauga Library, taking out books like *Conversations with God*. This book, and others, stated that *humans* create and manifest our destinies. Manifesting seemed more tangible, more doable than just sitting around waiting for my dreams to come true, or praying to Sai Baba.

David Letterman David Letterman David Letterman David Letterman
David Letterman David Letterman David Letterman David Letterman
David Letterman David Letterman David Letterman David Letterman
David Letterman David Letterman David Letterman David Letterman
David Letterman David Letterman David Letterman David Letterman
David Letterman David Letterman David Letterman David Letterman
David Letterman David Letterman David Letterman David Letterman
David Letterman David Letterman David Letterman David Letterman

Many of my friends in Edmonton stopped responding to my emails, stopped returning my calls. My ex-girlfriend, Sabrina, was one of the few people who stayed in touch. One late night on the phone, she suggests that I move back home and write off this time in Toronto as a "failed experiment." Sabrina had always been so supportive of my music journey. But maybe she was right.

I call my mom and tell her that I'm thinking of moving home. I assume that she'll be overjoyed. Instead, she says to me, "But have you done what it is you needed to do?"

I say, "What do you mean?"

And she says, "I don't want you coming back home and being sad because you didn't do what you needed to do. If this is about the money, we will keep supporting you as best as we can."

This was such a profound act of generosity from my mother. I knew how much it had hurt her that I'd moved out, and yet here she was, telling me to continue to follow my dreams.

I start seriously looking for my own place in Toronto via Craigslist. I find a bachelor on Saint Clair West and Oakwood, and once I get there, I notice that it's in the centre of the holy trinity of No Frills, Blockbuster Video, and McDonald's. I sign the lease on the spot.

I call Grace, a woman I barely know. She had given me her number at a lesbian dance party one of the few times I had come into the city. She agrees to help me move out.

Grace shows up in Mississauga in her station wagon on a day that I know Mama Carla is going to be out of the house. I leave a note for Mama Carla saying, "*Thanks for everything,*" plus half a month's rent in cash. And then Grace and I, and my two suitcases and two boxes, escape onto the Gardiner.

A few weeks later, when I take Grace out for a thank-you lunch, she mentions in passing that she likes to photograph her poo. And thus, my friendship with Grace was short-lived.

THE SISTERS

Edmonton never brought in any big concerts, but now that I was living in Toronto, I could finally see all of my favourite artists. I also secretly hoped that these shows would be opportunities to be seen as a peer, or at the very least, an up-and-comer. Before every show I attended in 2003, I would tuck a copy of my CD into a manila envelope. Not *Throat* but my acoustic album, *Samsara: The Sketches*. I would scribble my email address and phone number on the back of the envelope and take it with me. During the show, I would wait for when everything would cut to black, and then I would hurl my CD onstage. For the rest of the show, I would watch only the lead singer's feet, hoping that they wouldn't accidentally or, perhaps deliberately, crush the CD. The next day, I would sit by my phone waiting for Jack White or Macy Gray or Sheryl Crow to call me. No one ever called.

Towards the end of the year, Sabrina sent me a show recommendation. Her new favourite band—a sibling duo from Alberta— was playing at Lee's Palace in November. She didn't have to sell me on it because I'd fallen in love with Tegan and Sara's latest album, *If It Was You*.

On the night of the show, I crank the album. I notice my CD on the dresser. I debate whether or not to bring it with me. It was the final show I was going to that year, and this was the last copy of my album. What did I have to lose? I grab my CD and head to Lee's Palace.

Halfway through the show, I boomerang my CD onstage. It almost hits Tegan's head. And yet, as Tegan walks offstage at the end of the show, she picks up my weapon of mass destruction and takes it with her.

A month goes by. I receive an email from Tegan. I nervously click on it. In the message, she tells me that she loves the album. She tells me that she would be happy to do anything she can to support me. The next day, she posts about me on the front page of the Tegan and Sara website. And a year later, they invite me to open for them on their US tour without ever seeing me perform live.

Holy shit! It worked! Sometimes you just have to throw your CD on the stage.

THE
RECORD DEAL

As soon as I was off the Tegan and Sara tour, I decided to buy an electric guitar to change my songwriting approach and a MacBook so that I could demo my songs. My fellow tourmate Rachael Cantu had shown me how to use GarageBand. Now I was able to record my vocals and my backup vocals, and experiment with drum loops and synth sounds. I was actually starting to realize the music I was hearing in my head.

Rachael also e-introduced me to her producer friend in LA, Meghan Toohey. I sent Meghan my new demos to show her exactly what I was imagining for my next album. It was a radically new sound for me—electro pop—inspired by artists like Goldfrapp and Peaches. When we officially started to work together, I would email Meg just my vocals. She would program beats and synths underneath and flip the track back to me. I would make notes and add sounds on my end, and we'd go back and forth until a song was finished. Thanks to technology and the internet, I was finally an active participant in the making of my music.

In 2007, I released this new album entitled *If We're Not Talking*. Even though it was my fourth album, it felt like it was my first. It was the first time I felt like I got the equation of the album right.

It was the first album I made that sounded less like the people I was working with and more like me. I told myself this was *the one*.

I started to receive positive reviews on dozens of music blogs. I was also on a new online platform called "MySpace" where I could share my music. Suddenly, I was getting instant, international feedback through enthusiastic comments, stream counts, and private messages ...

One message I received on MySpace was from a woman named Didi. Didi worked for an advertising company in Paris that was starting a boutique music label called KusKus. Apparently, Didi had discovered me on a music blog that had featured *If We're Not Talking* and my new electro cover of "Seven Nation Army." She was looking to sign just two acts. The first was an electro Beach Boys duo who wore matching Lacoste tennis clothes called "Housse de Racket." The second was going to be *moi*. Obviously, I thought this was a scam. But what was I going to do? Not respond?

After a few months of messaging back and forth, I found myself flying first class to Paris to meet Didi and perform my first European show. After years of playing in a city where the only way to get people excited about you was to be connected to Broken Social Scene or the Arts & Crafts label, I was shocked when the small Parisian lounge I was playing in filled up. The audience of young glamorous brunettes with bangs head-bopped and danced for my entire set, and cheered when I closed with "Seven Nation Army."

I couldn't have staged a better first impression for Didi and the label.

A month later, I signed with KusKus. I was now part of the great Canadian tradition of artists finding success first outside our home country. Canadians just didn't get me. They were too limited, too conservative—unlike the French.

The deal included a commitment to release two singles from *If We're Not Talking* with remixes by hot Euro DJs. This would be followed by a new album. All of these would be stocked at the trendsetting Paris shop Colette. KusKus's parent company would look for placements in ads and movies for my music. The deal also came with a $30,000 advance. Despite $11k going to my lawyer to broker the deal, I was thrilled to give my parents a sum in gratitude for co-signing the loan to pay for *Throat*. I was now also able to make a giant payment on this loan.

Upon signing, Didi said to me, "You're going to be bigger than Mika." And I believed her. Anyone remember Mika?

The first order of business was … changing my MySpace profile image. Didi said I didn't look masculine enough. This surprised me because a) I had a full beard in the photo and b) all the men in Paris seemed super gay to me.

During my next trip to Paris, she set up a photo shoot with a well-known older married couple photographer team. When I looked at the contact sheet, all the photos had a soft haze, making me look like a brown cherub. When Didi saw them, she said, "*Parfait!* You look like a *man*."

Later, we went to her office so that she could play me one of the remixes she had commissioned for my first single. I couldn't tell if it was any good. Didi said, "People are going to lose their shit." But when we released the remix, we received zero media coverage or any other major interest.

I kept my focus on the next album and began sending my new demos to the label. I was excited to share my heavier electro sound. Didi would take weeks to respond, and when she did, I would get messages like, "These are interesting, but do you have anything more like 'Seven Nation Army'? Or maybe more like Mika?" I would go back to the drawing board and submit another round of demos, and then another round and another round, and eventually, she just stopped responding. After months without contact, I finally heard from her that the label had decided not to release the second single. "This will give us more time to focus on the album."

Between the disconnect and pressure around my image, the stalemate with my music, and the label refusing to meet contractual obligations, I started to feel the way I felt in Mama Carla's apartment. One day over the phone, Didi hints, "It would be so great if you could be in Paris more often. It would really help with the budget." I tried to imagine myself selling baguettes in a Parisian café, trying to make it. Was I ready to give up stable employment, carry my *Throat* debt across the ocean?

Eighteen months after I signed with KusKus, eighteen months after they had told me that they were going to make all of my dreams come true, I used the balance from my advance to pay my lawyer to get me out of the contract. When it was all said and done, from the $30,000 I had received, my lawyer ended up profiting the most—making roughly $20,000.

I started plotting the independent release of my new songs, the ones Didi had rejected. I was back to square one. Except, not quite.

I was twenty-eight, and with thirty looming in the distance, the confidence of my twenties was beginning to fade. I had always believed that at some point my talent coupled with hard work would result in success. Like the good white people around me, I believed in a meritocracy.

But at the core of that belief is a deep sense of entitlement. Mama Carla's words came back to me. Who the fuck did I think I was, when there were thousands of artists who were more talented than me, with better voices than me, who were better looking than me? Who the fuck did I think I was?

Suddenly, a new doubt began to creep in: What if I didn't make it?

As I wrestled with this possibility, I felt profoundly rejected—but not by the industry or an imagined audience. I felt rejected by music. Betrayed by music. Unloved by music. Why didn't music love me back?

Music Ur the 1 (reprise)

I learned to sing to please my mother
I learned to sing to please God
I learned to sing to please the pretty girls

But along the way
I fell in love
With music

In a typical music biography, my character is supposed to get super full of myself, super trashy, super high on drugs, super suicidal, culminating with a grand redemption. But these things only happen *after* the skyrocket success. What happens if a star *isn't* born? No songs on the radio. No screaming fans. If there is no giant success, then there is only giant failure.

So what would success have looked like for me? The answer to that question is a moving target, often shaped by age, circumstance, and perspective. So let's go back to the beginning.

A young boy ascends from his body and becomes God after learning 300 bhajans.

A shy teenager morphs into a blonde ambition and is crowned champion of Youth Talent Quest.

An adolescent's debut record takes over the Euro charts and wins a Grammy.

An acclaimed adult popstar performs on the David Letterman show.

Instead, I stand before you now. Still human. A thirty-nine-year-old "writer." Sometimes a "visual artist," or even "filmmaker." A few might know me as a "musician"—someone who plays music. But I'm never known for a specific hit song or album I've recorded. Instead, I am mostly known for my collaboration with white artists.

And so I've failed at becoming a popstar.

I know. Naming failure is uncomfortable. This might be why someone naming their failure is often met with a well-intentioned assertion: "You haven't failed! Look at all the amazing things you've done!"

But I *have* failed at becoming a *popstar*.

And I know that naming failure is being ungrateful. Because wanting more is selfish. It's materialistic. "Ambition" is a dirty word. But I am ungrateful. I am all these dirty words. Because I would trade any accolade or achievement to be seen as a popstar. Or even just a one-hit wonder.

I have failed at becoming a popstar. And here is a list of forty reasons why:

I was born in Edmonton.

I was born in 1981.

My parents are immigrants.

No one invested a million dollars in me.

I'm not related to anyone famous.

I didn't fuck anyone famous.

I don't have mass sex appeal.

I don't own leather pants.

I am brown.

I am whitewashed.

I didn't embrace the sitar on my album.

I'm brown and queer.

I'm brown and queer and trans.

I don't know how to wear heels.

I don't have abs.

I don't have breasts.

I have chest hair.

I wore braces until I was twenty.

I'm an introvert.

I don't drink.

I don't do drugs.

I'm bad at networking.

I care too much about what people think.

I didn't work with the right people.

I didn't ask for feedback on my demos before recording them.

My manifestation powers are weak.

I secretly didn't want it bad enough.

I didn't move to Paris.

I created a backup plan by working a day job throughout my twenties and thirties instead of prioritizing my art.

I didn't study music.

I didn't fully commit to learning guitar or piano.

I didn't tour enough.

I didn't rehearse hard enough before all of my shows.

I'm slow at learning choreography.

I didn't audition for *Canadian Idol.*

I made the wrong song choices at Youth Talent Quest.

My songs aren't catchy enough.

I didn't have vocal training.

My voice isn't pleasant.

I never had the range.

But here's the thing. Despite this list, and despite my many attempts to put my desire for pop stardom in a box and hide it under the bed, I can't make the box, the desire, the ache, the dream go away.

So how do I continue to live with my dream alongside failure?

Showing Up

We didn't quite make it
But we didn't quite break it

It's easy to walk away
Just as easy to stay

Both sides have their merits
But in any marriage
You gotta keep showin' up—that's the work
You gotta keep showin' up

So with every note I sing I'm showin' up
Not sure what it means but I'll keep on showin' up
I might never sing outside this room
For anyone other than you
But that's enough
As long as I keep showin' up.

CREDITS

How to Fail as a Popstar
A Canadian Stage Production Commissioned by Canadian Stage
February 18–March 1, 2020
Upstairs Theatre

Play and Original Songs Written and Performed by Vivek Shraya

Director
Brendan Healy

Assistant Director
Clare Preuss

Set and Costume Designer
Joanna Yu

Lighting Designer
C.J. Astronomo

Associate Lighting Designer
Imogen Wilson

Music Composition and Sound Designer
James Bunton

Stage Manager
Jessica Severin

Apprentice Stage Manager
Kimberly Moreira

Choreographer
William Yong

Head of Wardrobe
Ming Wong

Wardrobe Coordinator
Allie Marshall

Cutter
Marlee Bygate

Head of Properties
Mary Spyrakis

Head Technician
Jon Cunningham

AFTERWORD

In the summer of 2011, I saw Liz Peterson and Sean O'Neill's play *Express Yourself* in a small upstairs theatre on Ossington Avenue in Toronto, as part of SummerWorks Festival. I had no idea what to expect but was intrigued by the promotional image and, of course, the Madonna song title. For the entirety of the show, I was enthralled by Liz's storytelling, which seamlessly weaved into song and dance, as though, for her, all the mediums she was employing were one. There was also a projection element that included real-time live footage of her performing, captured by Sean, who moved in and out of the audience. I left the play feeling energized and convinced that theatre could hold and blur the multiplicity of my own art practice, and of me.

A few years later, I invited then–artistic director of Buddies in Bad Times Theatre, Brendan Healy, to participate in my short film *What I LOVE about being QUEER*. We stayed in each other's orbit through Facebook and our involvement in Toronto's queer arts communities. Eventually, we began to discuss possible opportunities to work together again, this time in theatrical contexts, but the ideas and the timing were never quite right.

In the summer of 2018, I was working on my second novel, *The Subtweet*, which is set in the music industry. Writing about music, expressing in words what a song is conveying through sound, is an underrated art—a thoughtful album review or interview with a musician can deepen the intimacy between a music listener and the music itself by offering a clarifying, affirming, or even alternate perspective. I began reading music biographies as a way of developing my music writing skills.

One biography, *The Emperor of Sound: Timbaland*, had a particular impact on me, and not just because I am a huge fan of his thumping, hypnotizing production skills. I was engrossed by stories about how Timbaland wrote Ginuwine's "Pony" and how Missy Elliott was his ultimate muse and cheerleader. I was fascinated by the details that enabled me to fill in the gaps in my understanding of his creative process from a time when artists and information about their lives and their work were far less accessible.

This book, and other music biographies I read, also evoked memories of my own music journey, and I started to imagine writing my music autobiography. But I quickly realized that my story lacked the main ingredient of this genre: mainstream success. What makes music biographies like Timbaland's so compelling are the recognizable milestones of their careers. You might not know much about Timbaland himself, but most people are familiar with the many artists he has elevated, like Justin Timberlake and Aaliyah, and the hits he has produced, like "Cry Me a River" and "Big Pimpin'."

My music career has reached none of the touchstones of popularity. I began to wonder how to tell an *anti*-success story. The title *How to Fail as a Popstar* quickly came to my mind. By this time, Brendan had become the artistic director at Canadian Stage. I pitched him the idea on a Sunday morning in July 2018, and the following year we began workshopping the play.

In our early conversations, I explained that it was essential that the story exposed and stayed anchored in failure. I didn't want to explore the ways failure can be generative, or show how "When one door closes, another opens." Instead, I wanted to create a play that expressed the pain of facing a closed, locked door, an unfulfilled dream. I also wanted to create a play that invited audience members to exhale as they confronted their own failures, admitting that perhaps they had traded in their big dreams for smaller ones, and that this downgrade of desires hurt. The necessity of this focus on failure was validated for me every time someone, after hearing or reading the title of the play for the first time, raced to "comfort" me with comments like "Never say never!" or undermine my claim to failure by listing, *to me*, my achievements in other fields. This is because acknowledging failure puts our ideas and expectations about investment (and returns), merit, destiny, and even God into question and, evidently, turmoil.

I am all too familiar with the process of writing alone in front of an aloof computer screen, so I told Brendan that I wanted the experience of writing this play to be more dynamic. To start, he sent me a number of prompt exercises about various events or stages in my music career. I responded to these prompts vocally, walking in circles in my kitchen, dictating my thoughts and stories on my phone. I would record a response to each prompt at least three times, curious to see what details would get lost, added, and embellished in my retellings. I assembled the first draft of the play by editing together the strongest components of these dictation sessions.

Because the play is about my relationship with pop music, I knew that it had to be bursting with music. Not just pop covers but also original songs. Before we began workshopping, I didn't know how many songs to write (with characteristic ambition, I initially planned for ten original songs, until I realized this would result in a very long play) or where to place them. I wanted the play to have elements of a musical, but I didn't want the songs to feel overly forced or contrived in that "Not another song!" kind of way. I decided that, as a baseline, the show would classically open and end with a song. Given that this was a love story, the opening song would be about falling in love with music, and the closing song would be about breaking up. "Music Ur the 1" and "Showing Up" were born from these guidelines, the latter composed through tears in the shower. "I'm a fag 4 U," which I had written earlier with the intention of using it in two other projects, found its rightful home in this play—a reminder to hold on to and be patient with every creation because you never know when it will find its place to shine. "I Won't Envy 2.0" is a remodelled version of a song from my 2007 album, *If We're Not Talking*. Together, these four original songs form the heart of the play.

The experience of workshopping the play in the summer of 2019 was simultaneously invigorating and gruelling. Although I regularly explored challenging themes in my work, I started to realize how much the act of creating alone shelters me in my process. I have the room I desire to be able to finesse a sentence or a melody until I am satisfied that it is presentable. But in workshop, changes to the script were suggested and tested immediately and under the scrutiny of others. Working with Brendan, as well as Tawiah M'carthy and Mel Hague, who generously sat in during table reads and offered feedback, was like working with editors in real time, without the distance that allows me to slowly work through track changes at my own pace, by myself. Once dance choreography was added to the sessions (with William Yong), I learned that I did *not* have latent dance skills, and that, if anything, my moves were often stiff and clunky. But I also learned that all this spontaneity, though terrifying for a perfectionist like me, can yield unexpected results. The transformation of this play from the first draft to the full, tight version that now exists (in draft nine!) is a testament to this live, collaborative process.

It's fitting that while making a play about failure, I so often *felt* like a failure. But I think one of the reasons this play now feels like a major artistic achievement and highlight is because of my willingness to laugh at myself, to fully lay my guard down at the altar of Theatre, and to try to follow the intuitions and guidance of the dedicated and experienced creatives around me.

When the play finally opened in 2020, I had the luxury of performing it a total of sixteen times in Calgary and Toronto. "Luxury" is a potent and deliberate word choice here. It was a luxury to be able to offer an audience this complete marriage of my various artistic skills in beautiful theatre spaces. It was a luxury to have the assistance of a team who, every day, anticipated my needs before I named them, who managed the lighting and sounds, tuned my guitar, warmed and set my tea, ironed my costume and washed my theatre-designated underwear (some things about theatre remain a mystery!). Being supported like this, in a way I had never been before, granted me the luxury of being an *artist*, being able to focus on giving myself fully to the performance—which I did. There wasn't a single night when I didn't want to perform. Night after night, I went onstage and sang and cried devotedly, honouring the teenage boy who believed in pop music as holy, as exodus, as connection, and whose desire for pop stardom was all consuming and unrequited. Night after night, I aimed to share this boy's joy, heartache, and passion with the audience.

"Luxury" is an especially relevant word as I write this now, six months into the coronavirus pandemic. In many ways, the months since March 2020 have felt like a different kind of failure or writeoff—a collective mourning for what might have been and what will never be. My play was one of the last to be shown at Canadian Stage. Theatre seasons across the world were cancelled shortly after my show finished, and the closures have been extended through the fall and, in some cases, even the winter. It astounds me to think of a not-so-distant time when I had the luxury of performing in rooms filled with more than 100 people, sitting together in the middle of winter, not socially distanced and mask-free.

I miss that time immensely. Maybe the impact of the coronavirus and the lockdown has caused me to over-romanticize, but I often think of the *Popstar* run as the best time of my life. I'm not sure when, or if, this play will ever be performed again. But I am grateful that, for now, it exists here, in book form, as a memento in honour of the stories of failures that are never expressed or published, and of a time when a story of failure brought us together.

Vivek Shraya
September 2020

ACKNOWLEDGMENTS

A special thank-you to the early supporters of my popstar dreams: Shamik, Mom, Katherine, Shemeena, Elise, Ben, Greg, and Tegan and Sara.

Thank you to Brendan for seeing the value in failure.

Thank you to Canadian Stage, Arsenal Pulp Press, Adam, Trish, James, Mel, Tawiah, Dahlia, Bif, Owen, Elvira, Denise, High Performance Rodeo, the Alberta Foundation for the Arts, and the Canada Council for the Arts.

Thank you to every single person who has attended the play— there would be no show without you.

VIVEK SHRAYA is an artist whose body of work crosses the boundaries of music, literature, visual art, film, and theatre. Her books include *I'm Afraid of Men*, *The Subtweet*, *even this page is white*, and *The Boy & the Bindi*, and her album *Part-Time Woman* was longlisted for the Polaris Music Prize. She is one half of the music duo Too Attached and the founder of the Arsenal Pulp Press imprint VS. Books. A six-time Lambda Literary Award finalist, Vivek was a Pride Toronto Grand Marshal, was featured on the *Globe and Mail*'s Best Dressed list, and has received honours from the Writers' Trust of Canada and the Publishing Triangle. She is a director on the board of the Tegan and Sara Foundation and an assistant professor of creative writing at the University of Calgary. Vivek is currently adapting her debut play, *How to Fail as a Popstar*, into a television pilot script with the support of CBC. *vivekshraya.com* | *@vivekshraya* | *#popstarplay*

Original songs from *How to Fail as a Popstar*
are available on all digital platforms.